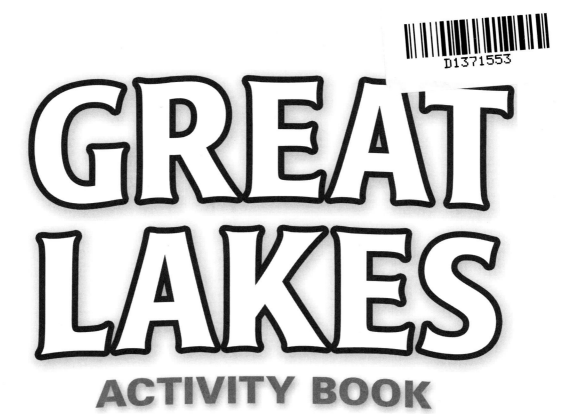

GREAT LAKES
ACTIVITY BOOK

by Paula Ellis

illustrations by Shane Nitzsche
with Anna Christenson

Dedicated to my great family, great friends
and great times on the Great Lakes.
                              ~Paula

Cover design by Ryan Jacobson
Book design by Lora Westberg

10 9 8 7 6 5 4 3 2

Copyright 2015 by Paula Ellis
Published by Adventure Publications
820 Cleveland Street South
Cambridge, Minnesota 55008
1-800-678-7006
www.adventurepublications.net
Printed in U.S.A.

ISBN: 978-1-59193-526-1

D1371553

Welcome to the Great Lakes

The area that's now home to the Great Lakes was once covered by giant glaciers. About 20,000 years ago, the land began to warm and the glaciers started melting and moving away. Large basins and rivers formed and were filled with water from the melting ice. Today, the Great Lakes contain about 20% of all the surface fresh-water supply in the world. That's about six quadrillion gallons, enough to cover the whole continental United States in almost 10 feet of water!

American Indians moved into the area about 10,000 years ago. In contrast, European explorers arrived about 400 years ago (around the 1600s). Some were looking for a way to the Pacific Ocean. The explorers set up trading posts and church missions around the Great Lakes. Voyageurs (French-Canadian travelers) and other traders paddled their birch-bark canoes over the waters of the lakes and rivers. They traded their blankets, tools and other goods to American Indians in exchange for animal furs.

Fishermen came to the Great Lakes to take advantage of the many fish living in the waters. Loggers harvested the area's trees in order to build homes for people coming to settle the land.

Today, the five Great Lakes—Lake Superior, Lake Michigan, Lake Huron, Lake Erie and Lake Ontario—are connected by waterways, from the Midwest all the way to the Atlantic Ocean. Goods like coal, iron ore, cement, corn, wheat and more are shipped from Lake to Lake and, eventually, around the world.

About 35 million people live in the Great Lakes area, including Canada and the US. They depend on the lakes for drinking water and as a water highway to transport goods in and out of the region by ship. Furthermore, many people rely on the Great Lakes for jobs, such as the sailors who work on the giant ships.

Each year, millions of people visit the Great Lakes to vacation and to delight in activities like fishing, boating, swimming, camping and snowmobiling. Welcome to the Great Lakes. Enjoy this book, and learn about fun and exciting things that make the Great Lakes great!

What do you want to do on the Great Lakes?

- ☐ spot a ship
- ☐ cross a bridge
- ☐ catch a fish
- ☐ swim in the water
- ☐ see a moose
- ☐ build a sand castle
- ☐ find a pretty rock
- ☐ run down a sand dune
- ☐ visit a lighthouse

Great Lakes Map

Use the map to find the answers.

What country is on the northern border of the Great Lakes?

☐ Mexico   ☐ France   ☐ Canada   ☐ Norway

How many states border the Lakes? (hint: Canada is not a state.)

☐ Five   ☐ Eight   ☐ Nine   ☐ Twelve

Which states border the Great Lakes?

☐ North Dakota   ☐ Montana   ☐ Illinois   ☐ Wisconsin
☐ Pennsylvania   ☐ Kansas   ☐ Michigan   ☐ Missouri
☐ New York   ☐ Iowa   ☐ Ohio   ☐ Indiana
☐ Kentucky   ☐ Minnesota   ☐ Nebraska   ☐ Virginia

(answers on page 62)

ABCs of the Great Lakes

Take a trip through the alphabet on the Great Lakes.

A is for **Agates**, beautiful gemstones found in the Great Lakes region.

B is for **Buffalo**, a large city in New York and a Lake Erie port.

C is for **Canada**, the country that shares the Great Lakes with the US.

D is for **Jim Dreyer**, who swam across all five Great Lakes.

E is for **Erie Canal**, a waterway that connected Lake Erie to the ocean.

F is for **Freshwater** in the Great Lakes that connects to the salty ocean.

G is for **Glaciers** that melted and helped to form the Great Lakes.

H is for **Hiawatha**, who's said to have united the Iroquis peoples.

I is for **Inland Seas**, another name for the sea-sized Great Lakes.

J is for **Jigs**, lures used by fishermen out on the Great Lakes.

K is for **Keweenaw**, a Michigan peninsula that juts into Lake Superior.

L is for **Lumberjacks**, who cut down trees along the Great Lakes.

M is for a **Sea Monster** named Bessie, which some say lives in Lake Erie.

N is for **Nets** that commercial fishermen use on the Great Lakes.

O is for **Oliver Hazard Perry**, who helped to win the Battle of Lake Erie.

P is for **Pictured Rocks National Lakeshore** on Lake Superior's south shore.

Q is for **Quagga Mussels**, clam-like invasive species harmful to the Lakes.

R is for **Regattas**, boat races held each year on the Great Lakes.

S is for **Saint Mary's River**, which connects Lake Huron to Lake Superior.

T is for **Tugboats** that push and pull giant ships around the harbors.

U is for **Underwater**, where trophy fish, shipwrecks and treasures hide.

V is for **Vacations** taken by people who enjoy the Great Lakes.

W is for **White Pine Trees**, cut down and shipped across the Great Lakes.

X is for **eXtreme Weather** that causes storms and giant waves.

Y is for **Yodel**, the call of a Common Loon heard on the Great Lakes.

Z is for **Zug Island**, a Detroit island made when a ship channel was dug.

Lake Erie

Lake Erie is the warmest and shallowest of the Great Lakes. About 11 million people who live near the Lake depend on it for their water supply. Fishermen from around the world come to Lake Erie to catch walleye. Some fishermen call it "The Walleye Capital of the World."

Help the fisherman get to Lake Erie, through both arrows, and find his way to catch a big walleye.

(answer on page 62)

Lake Huron

Lake Huron is named after the Huron Indians. The Lake is the second largest Great Lake by surface area, and it has more islands than any other Great Lake. One of its islands, Manitoulin Island, is the largest freshwater island in the world. Some 1,000 ships have sunk in Lake Huron.

 Draw several shipwrecks inside the waters of Lake Huron. Color the islands, too.

Lake Michigan

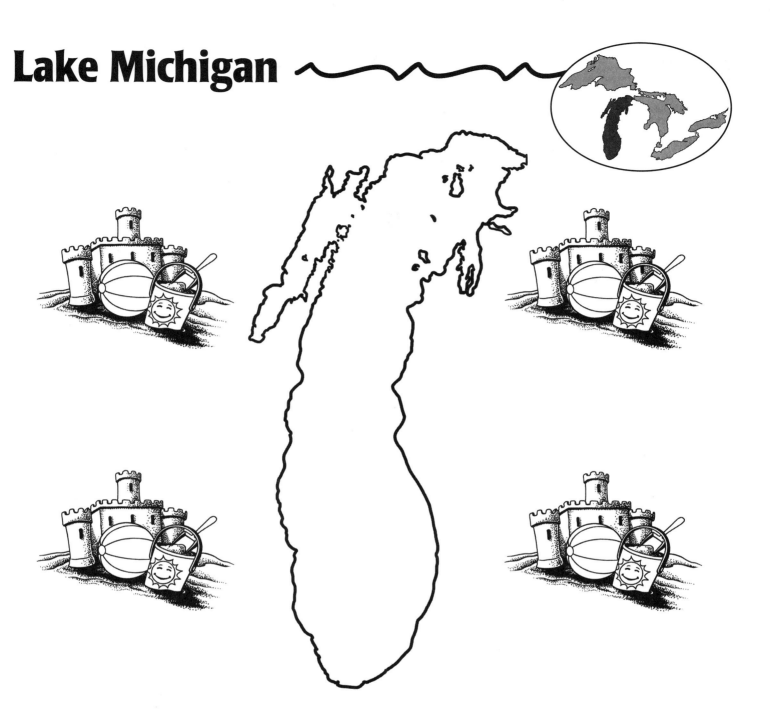

Lake Michigan is the third-largest of the five Great Lakes by surface area. It is the only Great Lake completely inside the United States. Visitors love the lake for its good fishing, sandy beaches and world famous sand dunes. An American Indian word for the lake is *Michi Gami*.

 Building sand castles is a fun activity on the beaches of Lake Michigan. Can you find the one that's different?

(answer on page 62)

Lake Ontario

1. Atlantic Ocean

2. _____

3. _____

4. _____

5. Lake Erie

Lake Ontario is the first Great Lake that ships reach from the Atlantic Ocean. From the ocean, ships travel through the Saint Lawrence River to Lake Ontario. To continue inland, the ships can sail through the Welland Canal toward Lake Erie. Lake Ontario is the smallest of the Great Lakes by surface area.

Read the text above, and then label the seaway from the Atlantic Ocean to Lake Erie.

(answers on page 62)

Lake Superior

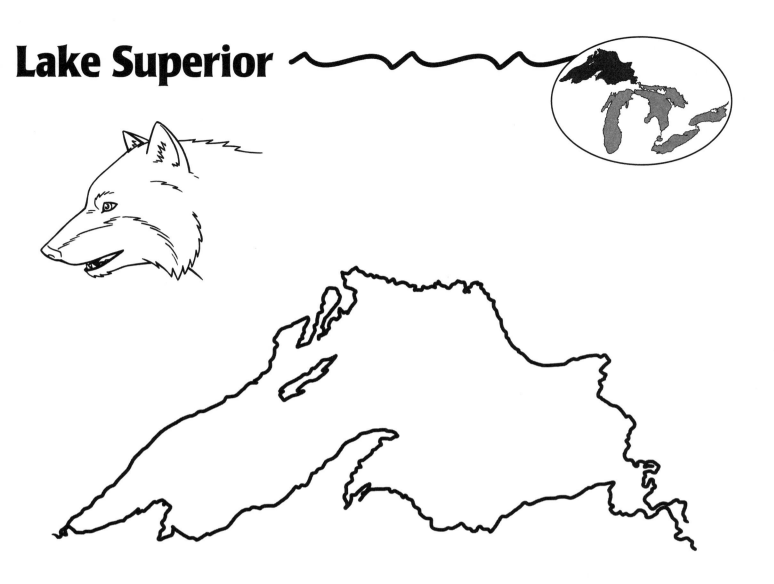

Lake Superior is the largest and deepest Great Lake. It holds more water than all the other Great Lakes combined. It is also the largest freshwater lake, by surface area, in the world. Lake Superior touches two countries, the US and Canada, and three states, Minnesota, Wisconsin and Michigan.

 Lake Superior is nicknamed the Wolf's Head. Color the Lake above to look like a wolf's head.

Scuba Diving

There are many different ways to explore the waters of the Great Lakes. All the shipwrecks at the bottom of the lakes make scuba diving a popular activity. Divers explore wrecks of lake freighters and other boats that sank many years ago. It's hard to count all the shipwrecks in the Great Lakes because many have not been found.

 Some people believe that there could be more than 20,000 shipwrecks in the Great Lakes!

Lighthouse Names

```
O N T O N A G O N P S O
O A K V I L L E W O E L
V C M A R B L E H E A D
L R C S S E L K I R K M
C I G H M L U I T E E I
A S U T B D I N E E V S
P P L A L I S G S F I S
E P P B L E G T H J C I
C O I U F P N B O T H O
H I N L V O E S A R H N
A N C A H X G N L Y M T
T T B E B I G S A B L E
```

ALPENA	CRISP POINT	ONTONAGON
ASHTABULA	KEVICH	OLD MISSION
BIG BAY	MARBLEHEAD	POE REEF
BIG SABLE	MCGULPIN	SELKIRK
CAPE CHAT	OAKVILLE	WHITE SHOAL

**Find the names of the lighthouses hidden in the word
find above. Look for bonus Great Lakes words too!**

(answers on page 62)

Isle Royale

There are thousands of islands in the Great Lakes, as many as 35,000. Isle Royale, in Lake Superior, is perhaps the most famous. It is a wilderness island and a national park. There are no roads on the island, only hiking trails—and about 1,000 moose, plus wolves and other wildlife.

 Moose are big, but they're also fast. At only five days old, a baby moose can already run faster than a person!

What Does Not Belong?

Color your favorite things about the Great Lakes. Draw an X over the things that do NOT belong in the region.

(answers on page 62)

American Indians

Ojibwe (Oh-jib-way), Ottawa (Ott-ah-wah) and Iroquois (Ear-uh-koy) are some of the American Indian tribes that lived near the Great Lakes since as far back as about ten thousand years ago. They used the region's waterways, including lakes and rivers, to travel and to catch fish to eat.

Guess which states were named for these American Indian words: *minni-sotah*, *meskonsing* and *ohi-yo*.

(answers on page 62)

Sault Ste. Marie Locks

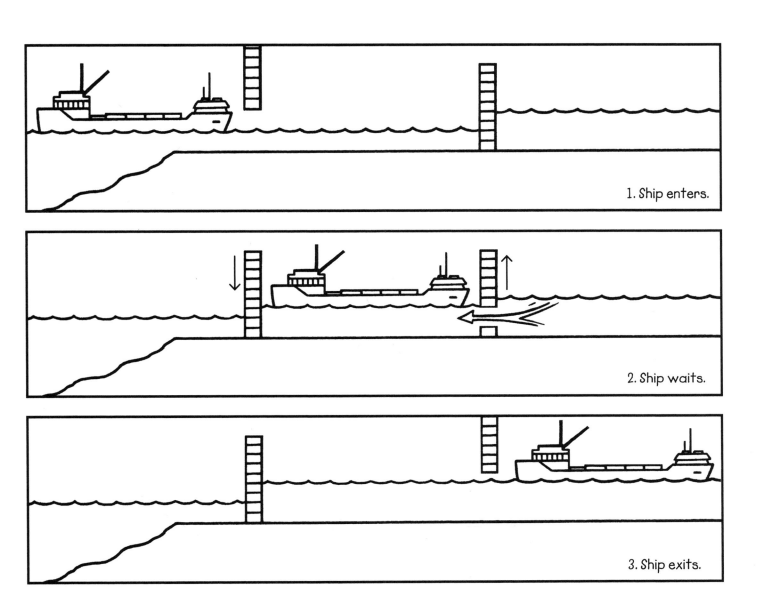

1. Ship enters.

2. Ship waits.

3. Ship exits.

Lake Superior is about 21 feet higher than Lake Huron, so the Sault Ste. Marie Locks, or the Soo Locks, were built to lift and lower the ships. A ship enters, and a gate closes behind it. Water flows into the lock to lift the ship or flows out of the lock to lower it. The next gate opens, and the ship proceeds.

More than 90% of the country's iron ore that's made into steel passes through the Soo Locks!

Ship Watching

You can tell a lot about a ship just by looking and listening. The smoke stack and ship colors show what company owns the ship. A flag on the back, or stern, of the ship says what country it's from. Boat horns are signals. One short horn means the boat is ready to move. Five short blasts mean danger!

 If you owned the ship above, what colors would it be? What country would the flag be from?

Sand Dunes

Millions of years ago, glaciers covered the Great Lakes area. When they melted, they left behind lots of sand. Over time, wind and waves helped to build huge sand dunes on the shores of Lake Huron, Lake Michigan and Lake Superior. Sleeping Bear Sand Dunes in Michigan are almost 450 feet tall!

 Fulgurites are crusty tubes of glass that are made when lightning strikes the dunes. Be careful of them!

Seaway Trail

Grab your camera—and binoculars, too—and take a hike! The Great Lakes Seaway Trail in northwestern Pennsylvania is a perfect place for bird watching. Along the trail, Presque Isle State Park is a peninsula in Lake Erie. It is a favorite spot for birds to feed and rest. More than 300 kinds of birds have been seen there.

Help the bird watcher follow the Seaway Trail, through the maze, to find the beautiful Ruffed Grouse.

(answer on page 62)

Surfing

Thanks to big winds and big waves, surfing has become a popular sport on the Great Lakes. Summer is a good time to surf, but the very best surfing happens during fall and winter, when storms create huge waves. Of course, surfing in winter gets very cold, so surfers wear special wet suits to keep themselves warm!

 During winter, surfers sometimes get icicles on their faces! They pour hot water on themselves to heat up.

Voyageurs

Voyageur (voy-yah-zhure) is a French word that means traveler. In the 1600s, 1700s and 1800s, voyageurs were people hired by companies to trade supplies for animal furs. Voyageurs paddled their canoes across lakes and rivers in the Great Lakes region, carrying furs from trappers and other goods from place to place.

 To save room in their canoes, the voyageurs sometimes didn't bring any dishes. They used their hats for bowls!

Piping Plover

The Piping Plover is a shorebird that likes sandy and gravel beaches. The dunes and lakefronts of the Great Lakes are ideal places for the birds to nest. Piping Plovers are an endangered species. That means so many are gone that soon there might be none left, so it's very important not to disturb the nests.

Piping Plovers are small, sand-colored birds. Connect the dots above to find out what one looks like.

Niagara Falls

Niagara Falls in the Niagara River is actually made up of three different waterfalls: American Falls and Bridal Veil Falls on the US side and Horseshoe Falls on the Canadian side. Power plants on the river use the rushing water to generate electricity for millions of people.

At night, the water is channeled into nearby power plants for electricity. This causes the falls to slow down!

What Makes the Lakes Great?

Across

3. Forms when lightning hits a dune
6. Great Lakes port farthest west
7. A man-made waterway
10. A type of iron ore
11. Many kinds live in the Great Lakes
12. Lands surrounded by water

Down

1. The Lakes' largest laker
2. A world port on Lake Erie
4. Their bright lamps warn ships
5. They melted to form the Lakes
8. You use it to cross above water
9. Collectible beach treasures

What makes the Great Lakes so great? Use the clues to fill in the squares above, and find out.

(answers on page 63)

Fun Words

Aft: at or near the back end of a boat or ship

Bow: at or near the front end of a boat or ship

Helm: the steering part of a boat or ship

Starboard: in the right direction of a boat or ship

Bitts: posts a ship is tied to, while docked, to keep it from moving

Buoy: a big bobber in the water that warns boats of danger

Port: in the left direction of a boat or ship

Taconite: iron ore that's found in certain rock and made into steel

Learning new words can be fun. Use these Great Lakes words to sound more like a sailor!

Chicago

Chicago is one of the largest cities in the US, and its famous Port of Chicago is located on Lake Michigan. Cargo, such as lumber, grain and goods from around the world, is brought to the Port of Chicago by ship and then transported to trains, trucks and riverboats that deliver the goods to inland parts of the country.

 More than 100 years ago, "Christmas Tree Ships" began coming at year's end, loaded with trees for the people!

Island Names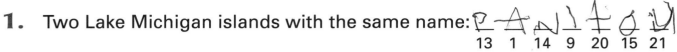

1. Two Lake Michigan islands with the same name: P A N I T O U
   13 1 14 9 20 15 21

2. P O L E E is the largest island in Lake Erie.
   16 5 12 5 5

3. S C A R E C R O W Island sounds like it should be in a garden.
   19 3 1 18 5 3 18 15 23

4. Great Blue Herons like to nest on D I C K I N S O N Island.
   4 9 3 11 9 14 19 15 14

5. Some think snakes lived on R A T T L E S N A K E Island.
   18 1 20 20 12 5 19 14 1 11 5

6. People from Iceland settled on W A S H I N G T O N Island.
   23 1 19 8 9 14 7 20 15 14

7. H E N Island has three islands around it called "Chicken" Islands.
   8 5 14

8. The US's largest freshwater island is D R U M M O N D Island.
   4 18 21 13 13 15 14 4

A	B	C	D	E	F	G	H	I	J	K	L	M
1	2	3	4	5	6	7	8	9	10	11	12	13

N	O	P	Q	R	S	T	U	V	W	X	Y	Z
14	15	16	17	18	19	20	21	22	23	24	25	26

 There are thousands of islands in the Great Lakes, and a few are listed above. Use the code to find the island names.

(answers on page 62)

Fish

Many kinds of fish live in the Great Lakes. Sunfish and perch are some of the smaller types of fish. However, sport fishing brings people from around the country to catch bigger fish, like whitefish, salmon, trout and sturgeon. What kind of fish have you caught or would you like to catch?

The walleye is named for its large, cloudy eyes. Connect the dots to find a walleye in the picture above.

Iron Ore

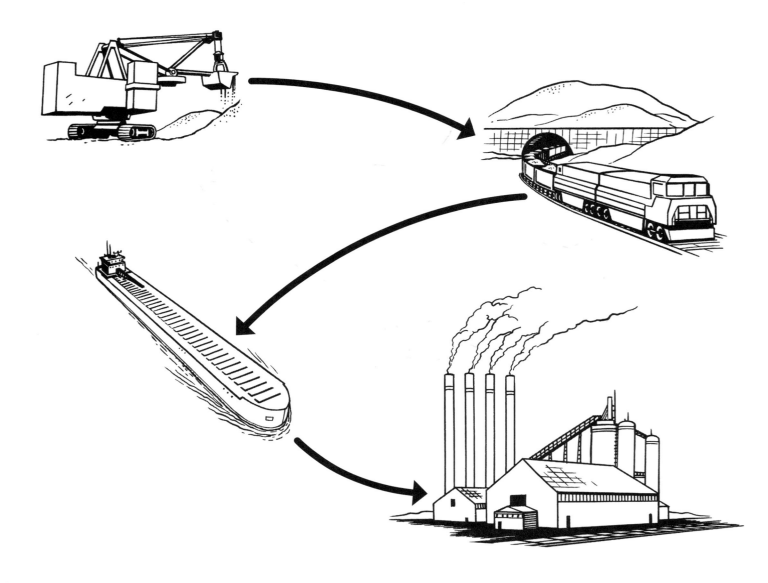

Millions of tons of grain, coal, stone and iron ore are shipped across the Great Lakes. Taconite, a kind of iron ore, is dug up, crushed into powder, processed and rolled into tiny balls. Trains take the ore to ships that deliver the ore to steel mills. The ore is then made into steel for buildings, cars, refrigerators and other products.

 Most of the boats on the Lakes are self-unloaders. That means they unload themselves with a moving belt!

Edmund Fitzgerald

Because the Great Lakes are such large bodies of water, the land around the lakes stays cooler in the summer and warmer in the winter. This helps to create some terrible storms that have caused countless shipwrecks. The *Edmund Fitzgerald* sank into Lake Superior during a storm on November 10, 1975.

There were 29 sailors on the *Edmund Fitzgerald* when it sank. Sadly, all of them went down with the ship!

US Coast Guard

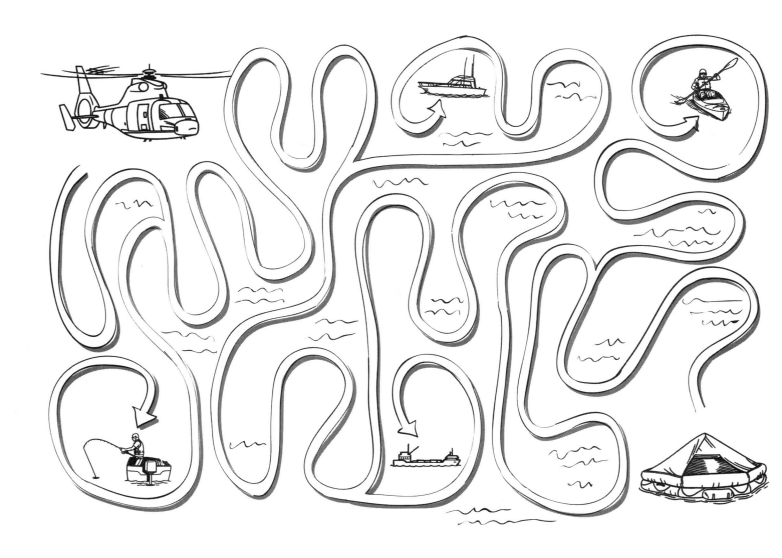

The United States Coast Guard is important to people's safety and protection on the Great Lakes. The sailors of the Coast Guard help people in trouble and make sure that laws are obeyed. They use helicopters and boats to rescue people in danger—and even icebreakers to rescue boats stuck in the ice.

Someone's in trouble! Help the Coast Guard helicopter find its way through the maze and to the life raft.

(answer on page 63)

Whitefish Point Lighthouse

Whitefish Bay, on Lake Superior, is a dangerous area because of wind, storms and waves. Hundreds of ships have sunk there. Whitefish Point Lighthouse was built to help guide ships though the dangerous water. It was one of the very first lighthouses built on the Lake, and it's the oldest active lighthouse on Lake Superior.

True or false? The steel tower on the lighthouse was built way back when Abraham Lincoln was President!

(answer on page 63)

31

Father Marquette

Father Marquette came to the Great Lakes, from France, in the early 1600s. He was a priest who lived among the American Indians. He learned their language, and he introduced them to the Christian religion. Father Marquette was also an explorer; he was one of the first Europeans to visit the area that we now call Lake Michigan.

 Roads, cities, counties, high schools, parks and even a university have been named after Father Marquette!

Laker

A lake freighter, or laker, is a ship on the Great Lakes that transports goods such as iron ore, grain, limestone, coal, salt and cement. Lakers do not go all the way to the ocean, though. The *Paul R. Tregurtha* is the largest laker on the Great Lakes. It's about as long as three football fields!

The *Paul R. Tregurtha* can carry about 150 million pounds—or the weight of 38,000 cars—in every load!

Duluth-Superior

Duluth is Minnesota's fourth-largest city, and Superior is Wisconsin's most northern big city. Together they make up the Twin Ports of Duluth-Superior, a very important shipping port on Lake Superior. The Duluth-Superior port is the largest, busiest and most western shipping port on the Great Lakes.

Duluth's Aerial Lift Bridge raises to let boats go under and lowers to let cars cross over the shipping canal!

Bridges

```
Q  G  O  A  R  A  I  N  B  O  W  Q
H  U  H  R  P  E  A  C  E  H  G  B
S  O  E  L  I  F  T  H  H  I  G  L
U  A  M  B  A  S  S  A  D  O  R  A
S  P  A  E  E  S  E  M  F  S  A  T
P  S  C  V  R  C  A  P  S  T  C  N
E  T  K  A  B  X  W  L  U  R  A  I
N  E  I  Y  N  A  A  A  P  E  B  K
S  E  N  M  W  A  Y  I  P  E  L  S
I  L  A  B  S  A  L  N  O  T  E  P
O  I  C  E  C  U  Y  K  R  J  V  A
N  O  B  L  U  E  W  A  T  E  R  N
```

AMBASSADOR	HOAN	PEACE
BAY	HOMER	QUEBEC
BLATNIK	ICE	RAINBOW
BLUE WATER	MACKINAC	SEAWAY
CHAMPLAIN	OHIO STREET	SKYWAY

Find the names of some Great Lakes bridges hidden in the word find above. Look for bonus bridge-themed words too!

(answers on page 63)

Tall Ships

Before freighters sailed on the Great Lakes, tall ships with massive sails moved goods (and people) around. Tall masts held big sails that allowed the wind to move the large wooden ships. Today these old-fashioned ships can be seen as they visit different ports during festivals along the Great Lakes.

The US *Brig Niagara*, a tall ship from the War of 1812, is now part of Pennsylvania's Erie Maritime Museum!

Lighthouses

More than 330 lighthouses have guided ships through the Great Lakes area. Their bright lights can warn ships of dangerous rocks and shallow water. When the weather is too foggy, captains can't see the lighthouses. Loud horns, called fog horns, warn of danger. Today, technology also helps ships travel safely.

Split Rock Lighthouse, on Lake Superior, only shines on November 10, in honor of the *Edmund Fitzgerald*!

Lakes and Land

Across

2. A well-known group of 22 islands
5. American Indian tribe of the Lakes
7. State with famous sand dunes
9. Lake known as the walleye capital
10. It helps ships get from lake to lake
11. The largest Great Lake

Down

1. Country that borders the Lakes
3. They're at the Lakes' bottoms
4. A popular trail for bird watchers
5. Great Lake nearest the ocean
6. New York port city on Lake Erie
8. Great Lake with the largest island

What do you know about the Great Lakes and the land around them? Use the clues to fill in the squares above.

(answers on page 63)

Island Mammals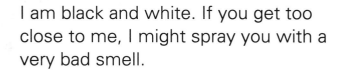

I am black and white. If you get too close to me, I might spray you with a very bad smell.

I am a great swimmer. I use my big, sharp teeth to cut down trees in order to build my home.

I am the largest member of the dog family. You might hear me howl in the night.

I like to climb trees and jump from branch to branch. I eat nuts, seeds and acorns.

I like to eat grass, moss and twigs. If I'm a male, I grow antlers. If I'm a female, I do not grow antlers.

Many of the Great Lakes islands are home to wild animals. Draw a line to match the mammals above with their descriptions.

(answers on page 63)

Fort Erie

The War of 1812 was fought between the United States and Great Britain. The US did not like the way the British treated American ships and its sailors. One of the war's biggest battles took place at Fort Erie on the Niagara River. Today, Fort Erie, one of many forts on the Lakes, is a historical museum

 Wars often have clear winners and losers, but after the fighting, both sides thought they won the War of 1812!

Rock Collecting

The Great Lakes have many different rocks because of the way they were created, millions of years ago. Agates on Lake Superior formed inside rock that was made of cooled lava. Petoskey stones on Lake Michigan are coral fossils from the warm ancient sea. Take a walk and look for beautiful rocks.

Many people polish the rocks they collect and display them, make jewelry out of them or even sell them!

Charter Fishing

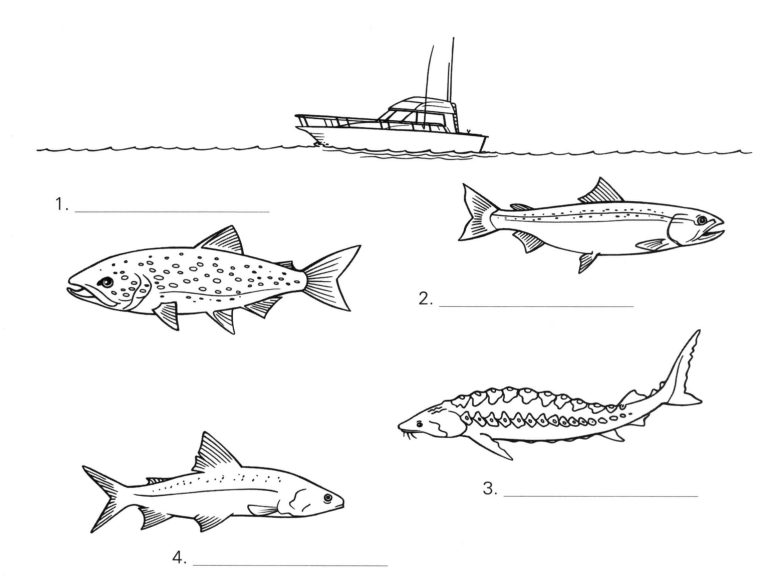

1. _____

2. _____

3. _____

4. _____

Charter fishing is a fun way to get out on the water. Professional fishermen know where the fish are, and they take customers on a fishing adventure. People love to reel in big fish like Coho Salmon (large mouth), Lake Sturgeon (whiskers), Lake Trout (large spots) and Lake Whitefish (small mouth).

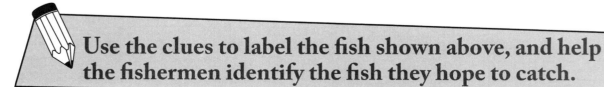

Use the clues to label the fish shown above, and help the fishermen identify the fish they hope to catch.

(answers on page 63)

Icebreaker

Winter brings ice to the lakes, and it causes problems for ships. They can no longer deliver their cargo. Icebreakers are boats that break through the thick ice on the lakes (and in the locks) to keep cargo ships moving. While icebreakers can prolong a shipping season, eventually the winter wins and the shipping season ends.

 When winter wind blows over warmer lake water, a "lake effect" can create a blizzard with several feet of snow!

Apostle Islands

The Apostle Islands are at the northern end of Wisconsin, in Lake Superior. This group of 22 islands is often called "the jewels of Lake Superior." Six lighthouses protect ships from the shallow water that surrounds the islands. Sailing and kayaking are popular ways to explore the beautiful area.

 The islands were named after the Bible's 12 apostles because it was first believed there were only 12 islands!

Protect the Lakes

Clean, healthy water is important to people, land, plants, fish and wildlife of the Great Lakes. For many years, people misused the Lakes. Factories dumped garbage in the water, and people left trash on the beaches. Laws were created to clean up the water and the land. Today, people work together to protect the Lakes.

Protect our Great Lakes for others to enjoy. In the picture above, cross out five things that hurt the area.

(answers on page 63)

Salt Mines

Millions of years ago, the area around Lake Erie was a saltwater sea. As the land warmed and dried, the saltwater dried up, and all the salt was left deep under the Lake. Today, the salt is dug out from 1,800 feet below Lake Erie. The salt is then processed and shipped by truck, train and boat to be used around the Great Lakes.

 In winter, snowplows spread salt on roads to keep them safe to drive on. The salt comes from below Lake Erie!

Fill in the Blanks

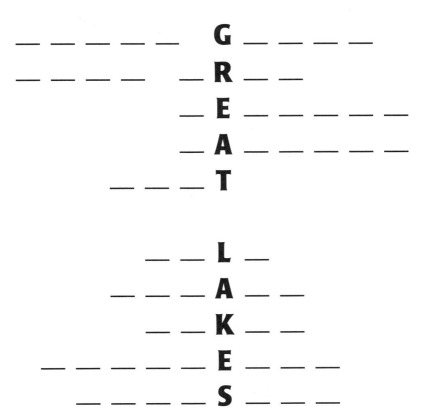

1. They protect people on the Lakes and make sure that they obey the law.

2. The warmest and shallowest of the Great Lakes.

3. This canal lowers ships from Lake Erie to Lake Ontario.

4. A fish named for its large, cloudy eyes.

5. The left direction, to a ship's captain.

6. Type of mines beneath Lake Erie.

7. Land that's completely surrounded by water.

8. This large type of boat does not go all the way to the ocean.

9. They were fur-trading travelers.

10. Stones made from coral fossils.

(answers on page 64)

Salty

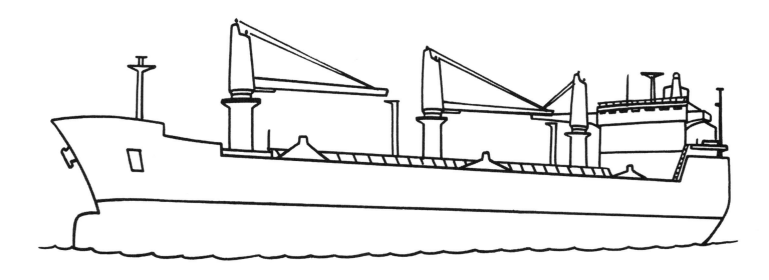

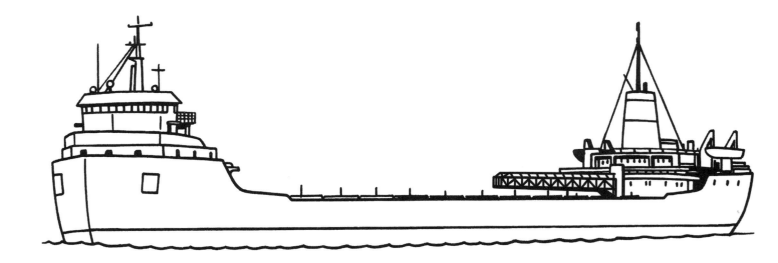

Ships that come to the Great Lakes from the Atlantic Ocean are nicknamed "salties." This is because ocean water is saltwater. Salties travel to the Great Lakes from countries around the world to get and to deliver cargo. Salties have big equipment, like cranes, on the deck, while lakers' decks look much flatter.

 Color the two ships pictured above. Circle the one that you think is a salty. How can you tell?

48

(answer on page 64)

Famous Names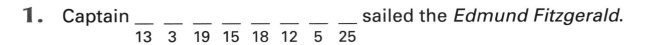

1. Captain __ __ __ __ __ __ __ __ sailed the *Edmund Fitzgerald*.
    13 3 19 15 18 12 5 25

2. Samuel de __ __ __ __ __ __ __ __ __ was a Great Lakes explorer.
    3 8 1 13 16 12 1 9 14

3. David __ __ __ __ __ __ __ __ designed famous Great Lakes bridges.
    19 20 5 9 14 13 1 14

4. Father __ __ __ __ __ __ preached to American Indians and miners.
    2 1 18 1 7 1

5. Chief __ __ __ __ __ __ __ fought against British invaders.
    16 15 14 20 9 1 3

6. *Le* __ __ __ __ __ __ __ was the first full-sized ship to sail the Lakes.
    7 18 9 6 6 15 14

7. Rene-Robert __ __ __ __ __ __ __ __ sailed in search of China.
    3 1 22 5 12 9 5 18

8. Etienne __ __ __ __ __ explored the Canadian side of the Lakes.
    2 18 21 12 5

<u>A</u>	<u>B</u>	<u>C</u>	<u>D</u>	<u>E</u>	<u>F</u>	<u>G</u>	<u>H</u>	<u>I</u>	<u>J</u>	<u>K</u>	<u>L</u>	<u>M</u>
1	2	3	4	5	6	7	8	9	10	11	12	13
<u>N</u>	<u>O</u>	<u>P</u>	<u>Q</u>	<u>R</u>	<u>S</u>	<u>T</u>	<u>U</u>	<u>V</u>	<u>W</u>	<u>X</u>	<u>Y</u>	<u>Z</u>
14	15	16	17	18	19	20	21	22	23	24	25	26

 **Great Lakes history includes many important names.
Use the code to discover the names to remember above.**

(answers on page 64)

Types of Fish

```
M  I  N  N  O  W  B  O  B  B  E  R
F  P  L  U  R  Z  L  A  K  E  C  L
I  I  S  E  M  S  U  N  F  I  S  H
N  K  W  H  I  T  E  F  I  S  H  T
C  E  W  C  A  D  G  H  O  O  K  R
A  A  O  R  S  D  I  P  J  V  L  O
T  F  R  A  W  A  L  L  E  Y  E  U
F  O  M  P  B  F  L  B  G  R  H  T
I  A  J  P  B  A  Q  M  A  L  C  J
S  T  U  I  C  I  S  C  O  I  V  H
H  S  M  E  L  T  W  S  X  N  T  Y
Z  F  C  A  P  T  A  I  N  E  R  W
```

BASS	CRAPPIE	SMELT
BLUEGILL	PERCH	SUNFISH
CARP	PIKE	TROUT
CATFISH	SALMON	WALLEYE
CISCO	SHAD	WHITEFISH

"Catch" the Great Lakes fish hidden in the word find above. Look for bonus words too!

(answers on page 64)

Mackinac Bridge

Bridges are important to the Great Lakes, since they allow people and vehicles to pass over the water. The Mackinac (mack-in-aw) Bridge is almost five miles long, and it connects the Lower Peninsula of Michigan to the Upper Peninsula of Michigan. Some Great Lakes bridges connect the US to Canada.

 Windsor Tunnel connects Michigan to Canada, but it goes under the Detroit River instead of over it!

Ferry

The Great Lakes are large bodies of water with few bridges. This makes it difficult to get across them. Ferries are important in transporting people, supplies, vehicles and even animals from place to place. When the Great Lakes freeze in winter, many ferries must stop until the ice melts in spring.

 Ferries are boats for cars. People can drive onto a ferry, ride across a lake, then drive off on the other side!

Boat Races

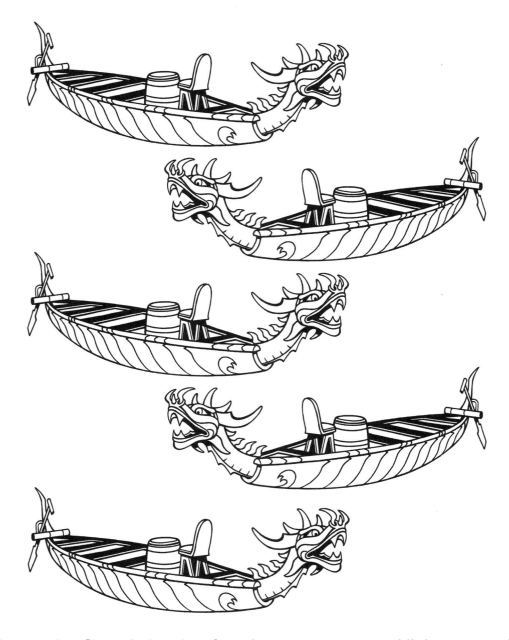

Boat racing on the Great Lakes is a favorite summer sport. High-powered speed boats and world-class sailboats from around the world compete in races on the Lakes. The oldest freshwater sailing race in the world is on Lake Michigan. The race is almost 300 miles from Chicago, Illinois, to Mackinac Island, Michigan.

Dragon boat racers paddle boats that look like dragons. Color the dragon boat that's different from the rest.

(answer on page 64)

Lake St. Clair

Lake St. Clair is part of the Saint Lawrence Seaway. It connects the Saint Clair River from Lake Huron to the Detroit River, which flows into Lake Erie. Lake St. Clair is so shallow that the middle of it had to be dug out, so the big ships could pass through. Michigan is on one side of the lake and Canada is on the other.

 As big boats move along the Detroit River, a mail boat delivers mail and even pizza to the sailors!

Ship Workers

Mariners, or sailors, on the Great Lakes can be away from home for days or weeks at a time. At port, there is a lot to do: from unloading cargo to loading supplies for the next trip. On the Lakes, repairs, maintenance, painting and other jobs keep the sailors working hard.

Many songs have been written about the courage and bravery of the Great Lakes sailors!

Bingo

If you see one of the people, places, animals or objects on the bingo card during your trip, mark it with an X. Be sure to mark the free space in the middle. If you get five Xs in a row, you win! Remember to yell "Bingo!"

B	I	N	G	O
GREAT LAKE	SALTY	SAND CASTLE	DEER	EXCAVATOR
FISHERMAN	WATERFALL	BRIDGE	TALL SHIP	SQUIRREL
LIGHTHOUSE	BIRD	FREE	PRETTY STONE	LAKER
SAILBOAT	SURFER	CAPTAIN'S HAT	BUS	KAYAK
BIG FISH	TRAIN	COAST GUARD	ISLAND	CYCLIST

License plate game: How many different state license plates can you find while traveling?

Cleveland

The Port of Cleveland is part of the city of Cleveland, Ohio, on Lake Erie. It is one of the biggest ports on the Lakes. Much of the cargo coming to the port comes from around the world, making it not only a Great Lakes port but a world port. This port was important for shipping steel, which helped in building railroads and bridges.

 Superman didn't come from the alien planet Krypton. The famous super hero was created in Cleveland!

Invasive Species

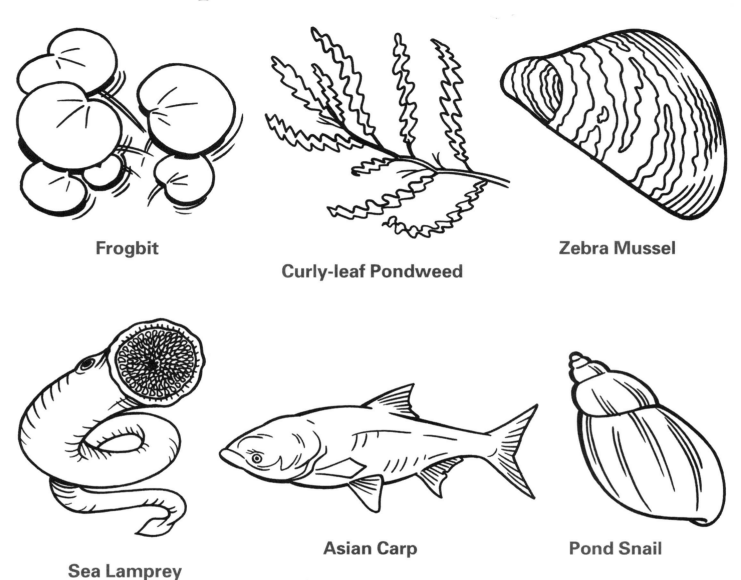

Frogbit

Curly-leaf Pondweed

Zebra Mussel

Sea Lamprey

Asian Carp

Pond Snail

Invasive species are plants and animals that aren't native to an area. When they arrive, they take food away from the plants and animals that are supposed to be there, and they can damage or destroy habitats. Laws have been passed to keep people and ships from accidentally bringing invasive species to the Lakes.

 A lot of invasive species were "hitchhikers." They got into the Lakes by attaching themselves to ships!

Water Safety Quiz

Although water can be fun, it can also be dangerous. Check the things below that will help to keep you safe around the water. Cross out the things that are dangerous.

- [ ] Take swimming lessons.

- [ ] Swim alone.

- [ ] Wear a life jacket.

- [ ] Always swim near the shore.

- [ ] Always tell someone where you are.

- [ ] Drink plenty of water.

- [ ] Don't wear sunscreen.

- [ ] Obey lifeguards and beach flags.

- [ ] Never swim during storms.

- [ ] Be careful around rocks.

- [ ] Never dive when you can't see the bottom.

- [ ] Swim with a buddy, instead of alone.

- [ ] Keep swimming, even if you get tired.

- [ ] Talk with your parents about when and how to call 9-1-1.

- [ ] Stay alert.

- [ ] Ignore signs that explain rules and offer warnings.

- [ ] If you get cold, take a break.

- [ ] Have fun with your family!

(answers on page 64)

Welland Canal

The Welland Canal is an important connection between Lake Ontario and Lake Erie. Without the canal, there would be no seaway from the Atlantic Ocean to the rest of the Great Lakes. Lake Erie is about 326 feet higher than Lake Ontario. Ships must pass through eight locks between the lakes.

It takes a ship about 11 hours to get through the 27-mile Welland Canal. A person could walk faster than that!

Great Questions

Are there whales in the Great Lakes?

No. Whales live in saltwater, like the ocean; the Great Lakes are freshwater, just like other lakes and rivers.

Why aren't the Great Lakes saltwater since they are connected to the ocean?

Water from the Great Lakes moves toward the ocean, not from it.

How much water is in all the Great Lakes?

About six quadrillion gallons. That's enough to cover the entire lower 48 US states in more than nine feet of water.

What's a good way to remember the names of the Lakes?

Think of the word **HOMES** for **H**uron **O**ntario **M**ichigan **E**rie **S**uperior.

How far is it from the Atlantic Ocean to Duluth, Minnesota?

About 2,038 nautical miles (or miles traveled on water). It takes about seven days to make the trip, depending upon the ship and the weather.

Is Lake Superior really the largest freshwater lake in the world?

It depends on how you measure it. Lake Superior is the largest by surface area, but Lake Baikal in Russia has more water in it because it's deeper.

Are they called boats or ships?

Usually, people call them "boats" if they stay on the Lakes. The ones that come from the oceans are called ships. All ships are boats, but not all boats are ships.

Where did the Great Lakes come from?

Legend says that the giant lumberjack Paul Bunyan walked across the area, and his footprints made the Lakes. What do you think of that?

Where did the Great Lakes really come from?

The land was once covered by giant glaciers. About 20,000 years ago, the land began to warm and the glaciers melted. That helped to form the Great Lakes.

Answers

Page 3–Great Lakes Map

1. Canada
2. Eight
3. Minnesota, Wisconsin, Michigan, Illinois, Indiana, Pennsylvania, Ohio, New York

Page 5–Lake Erie

Page 7–Lake Michigan

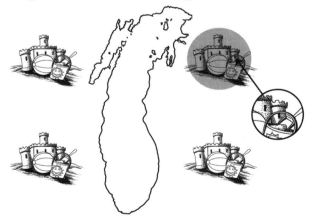

Page 8–Lake Ontario

2. Saint Lawrence River
3. Lake Ontario
4. Welland Canal

Page 11–Lighthouse Names

O	N	T	O	N	A	G	O	N	P		S				O	
O	A	K	V	I	L	L	E		W	O	E				L	
V		C		M	A	R	B	L	E	H	E	A			D	
L	C	R	C	S	S	E	L	K	I	R	K				M	
C	R	I	G	H	M	L	U	I	T	E	E	V			I	
A	I	S	U	T	B	D	I	N	E	E	F	I			S	
P	S	P	L	A	L	I	S	G	S	S	J	C			S	
E	P	P	P	B	L	E	G	T	H	F	H				I	
C	O	O	I	U	F	P	N	B	O	T					O	
H	I	I	N	L	V	O	E	S	A	R	Y				N	
A	N	N	C	A	H	X	G	N	L	Y	M					
T	T	T	B	E	B	I	G	S	A	B	L	E				

Page 13–What Does Not Belong?

Shark, palm trees, volcano, camel, whale, penguins

Page 14–American Indians

Minnesota (minni-sotah)
Ohio (ohi-yo)
Wisconsin (meskonsing)

Page 18–Seaway Trail

Page 26–Island Names

1. Manitou; 2. Pelee; 3. Scarecrow;
4. Dickinson; 5. Rattlesnake;
6. Washington; 7. Hen; 8. Drummond

Answers

Page 23—What Makes the Lakes...

Page 30—US Coast Guard

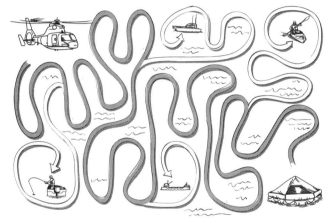

Page 31—Whitefish Point

True! The steel tower on the lighthouse was built in 1861.

Page 35—Bridges

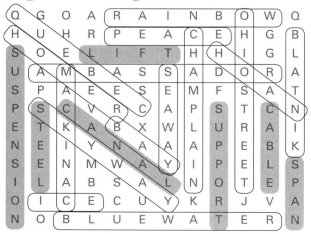

Page 38—Lakes and Land

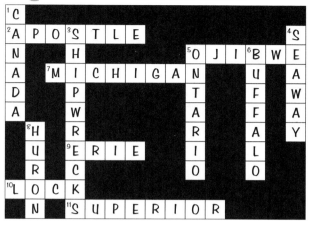

Page 39—Island Mammals

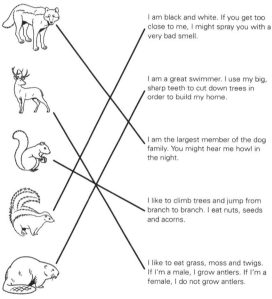

I am black and white. If you get too close to me, I might spray you with a very bad smell.

I am a great swimmer. I use my big, sharp teeth to cut down trees in order to build my home.

I am the largest member of the dog family. You might hear me howl in the night.

I like to climb trees and jump from branch to branch. I eat nuts, seeds and acorns.

I like to eat grass, moss and twigs. If I'm a male, I grow antlers. If I'm a female, I do not grow antlers.

Page 42—Charter Fishing

1. Lake Trout; 2. Coho Salmon;
3. Lake Sturgeon; 4. Lake Whitefish

Page 45—Protect the Lakes

trash on ground; plastic jug in river; fireworks; initials carved in tree; nails in tree; fire too close to trees; fire not in pit; fire not put out

Answers

Page 47—Fill in the Blanks

1. Coast Guard; 2. Lake Erie;
3. Welland; 4. Walleye; 5. Port;
6. Salt; 7. Island; 8. Laker;
9. Voyageurs; 10. Petoskey

Page 48—Salty

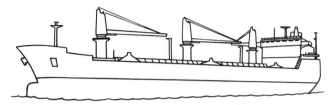

This one is the salty because there are large cranes on the deck.

Page 49—Famous Names

1. McSorley; 2. Champlain;
3. Steinman; 4. Baraga; 5. Pontiac;
6. Griffon; 7. Cavelier; 8. Brule

Page 50—Types of Fish

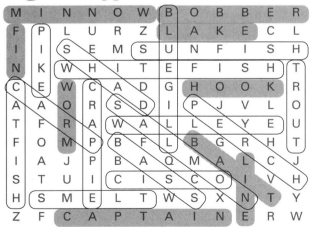

Page 53—Boat Races

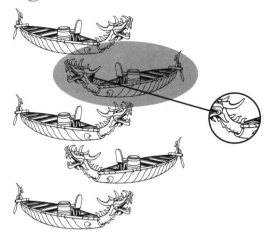

Page 59—Water Safety Quiz

- **X** Take swimming lessons.
- ☐ ~~Swim alone.~~
- **X** Wear a life jacket.
- **X** Always swim near the shore.
- **X** Always tell someone where you are.
- **X** Drink plenty of water.
- ☐ ~~Don't wear sunscreen.~~
- **X** Obey lifeguards and beach flags.
- **X** Never swim during storms.
- **X** Be careful around rocks.
- **X** Never dive when you can't see the bottom.
- **X** Swim with a buddy, instead of alone.
- ☐ ~~Keep swimming, even if you got tired.~~
- **X** Talk with your parents about when and how to call 9-1-1.
- **X** Stay alert.
- ☐ ~~Ignore signs that explain rules and offer warnings.~~
- **X** If you get cold, take a break.
- **X** Have fun with your family!